Triangle, Circle and Soul

Triangle, Circle and Soul

Harry Kretz

Geometry is knowledge of the eternally existent.
—Plato

Cover design: Daniel Nordaas and Claude Julien

ISBN 0-945803-73-7

The content of this book represents the view of the author and should in no way be taken as the official opinion or policy of Rudolf Steiner College or Rudolf Steiner College Press.

Book orders may be made
through Rudolf Steiner College bookstore:
Tel. 916.961.8729, Fax. 916.961.3032
Catalog and online orders: www.steinercollege.edu
Questions or comments,
E-mail: bookstore@steinercollege.edu

Rudolf Steiner College Press
9200 Fair Oaks Boulevard
Fair Oaks, CA 95628, U.S.A.

Soul

Soul: the rational, emotional, and volitional faculties in man conceived of as forming an entity distinct from the body.

—Funk and Wagnalls
Standard Desk Dictionary

I am especially grateful to Dennis Klocek, Norman Davidson, and Henrike Holdrege for their invaluable comments and suggestions.

Where was I? It seemed so real.

Draw a triangle, he said.

What kind of triangle should I draw?

Draw any triangle.

I thought a bit. Should I draw a triangle with three sides the same length, an equilateral triangle? That would look like this, only I would draw it larger.

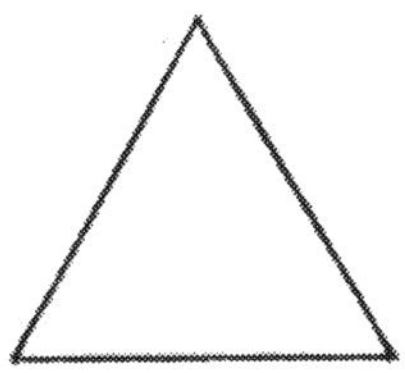

Fig. 1.
The equilateral triangle

Or should I draw a triangle with two sides the same length, an isosceles triangle?

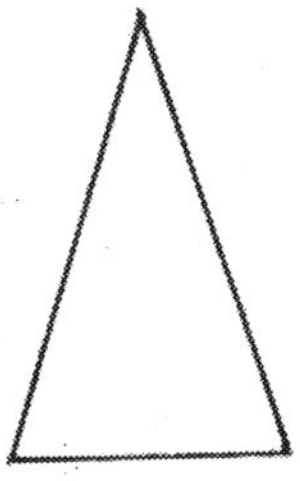

Fig. 2.
An isosceles triangle

Or should I draw a triangle with three sides each of different length, a scalene triangle?

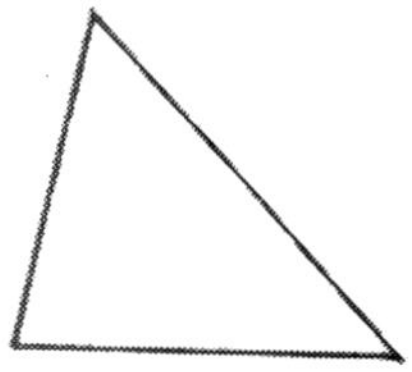

Fig. 3.
A scalene triangle

How about a triangle with one square corner, a right triangle?

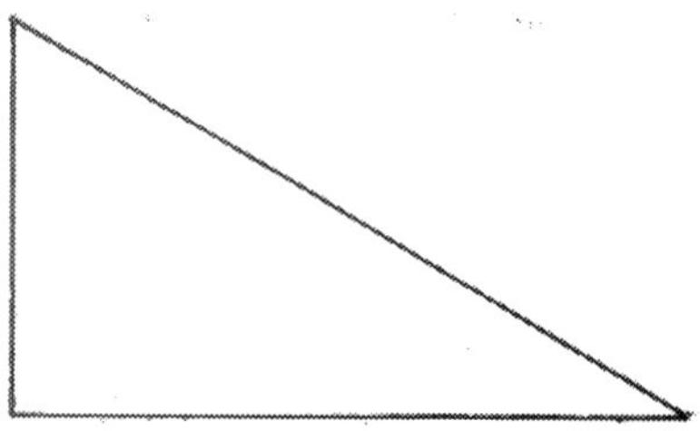

Fig.4.
A right triangle

Or a triangle with one angle larger than a square corner, larger than a right angle.

Fig. 5.
An obtuse triangle

And then again, it might be fun to draw a triangle that looks very different, like this, for example:

Fig. 6.
A long narrow obtuse triangle

Draw a triangle without thinking about it, he said.

So I drew a triangle and it turned out to be scalene. Each side was of slightly different length, not quite an equilateral triangle.

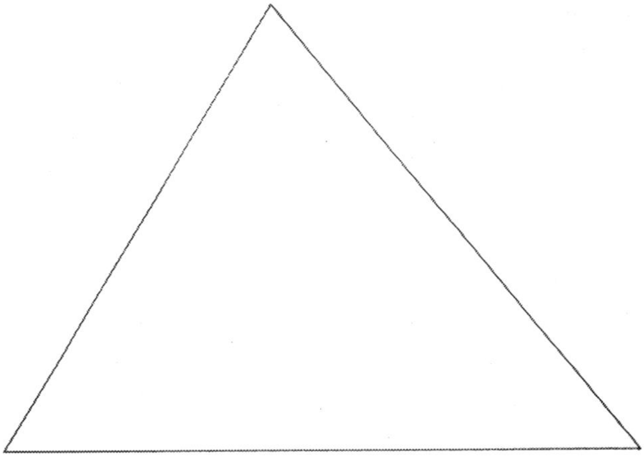

Fig. 7.
A scalene triangle

Good, he said. This triangle is symbolic of the present state of your soul, because it is you who drew it. Know that the soul is the bearer of the three fundamental capacities of thinking, feeling, and will. A dictionary might use the terms thinking, emotion, and volition. The long side symbolizes that capacity most highly developed. The short side, that capacity least developed. You decide which is which. Notice that all three sides are connected, each one to the other two.

I looked at the triangle. I am not evenly developed. But now I have to decide which soul capacity is symbolized by which side. Is the longest side symbolic of my thinking capacity towards which I have exerted myself? I have a college degree, if that means anything. But rather than thinking about the long side of the triangle, perhaps I should think about the short side. Could that short side symbolize my feeling life? I love my wife but she sometimes says that I am very critical. Do I love her, but love myself more? Or could that short side symbolize my will? I have accomplished much, though mostly what I wanted to do for myself. What needed doing for others was sometimes neglected. But what if the short side symbolizes my thinking, even with a college degree? I have to admit occasionally to having jumped to unfounded conclusions, which implies not thinking carefully. So, it looks as though all three soul capacities need to be worked on. And yet the shape of the triangle indicates a difference in development among the three.

You must be aware, he said, that the triangle you have drawn is fixed in shape on the paper while the soul configuration changes a little from time to time as you exert yourself toward clarity of thought, or nobility of feeling, or strength of will. Ultimately all three soul forces will approach a condition symbolized by the equilateral triangle.

Thank you, I said. That helps.

I pondered further. The three soul qualities are supposed to be interconnected, as each side of the triangle is connected to the other two.

Does thinking influence will? It must, because I decide what I want to do, and then do it.

Does thinking influence feeling? It must, because if I think he is a bad man, I might develop negative feelings toward him.

Does feeling influence thinking? If I love her, I will describe her in one way. If I don't, I may think of her in quite a different way.

Does feeling influence will? Certainly, if I love her I will do what she wishes. If I don't, I may find a reason to say, I'm busy right now.

Does will influence thinking? I thought about what I did and decided next time to do it differently.

Does will influence feeling? I accomplished what I set out to do and now I feel good about it. When I left it undone, another time, I felt guilty because I could have finished it.

So, it seems that all three, thinking, feeling, and will are interconnected as the three sides of the triangle are connected to each other.

Is this, I asked, what you had in mind when you spoke of the interconnectedness of the three soul qualities?

Yes, he said. It's a start. But now, find the center of your triangle.

How do I do that, I asked.

Here is how.

(As I was listening and drawing, it occurred to me that it might be a more satisfying, fulfilling experience for someone reading this, to pick up a circle compass, straight edge (ruler), pencil and several sheets of paper, and follow along, drawing according to the indications given, rather than just reading).

Using the straightedge, draw a triangle similar to mine but not exactly the same. We are all different but none of us is really so unbalanced as to have any one soul quality extremely unbalanced.

You need to draw a line, he continued, from the midpoint of each side of the triangle in the straightest possible way toward the interior. To start, select one side of the triangle and open your circle compass to any distance greater than half the length of that side. With the metal point at one end of the side, draw an arc. Keeping the same compass opening and metal point at the other end of that side, draw a second arc crossing the first arc in two places. Using the straightedge, draw a line that passes through the crossing of the two arcs. That line is called the perpendicular bisector. It crosses the midpoint of that side of the triangle, and makes a square corner with that side, hence, perpendicular.

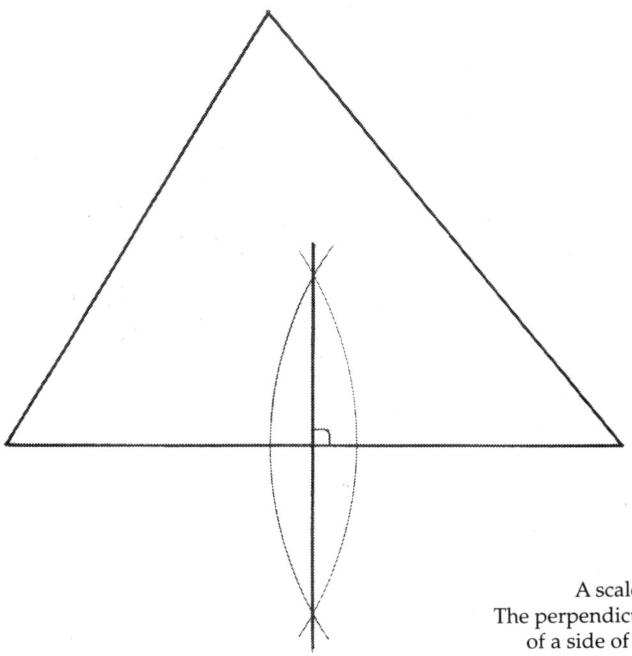

Fig. 8.
A scalene triangle.
The perpendicular bisector
of a side of the triangle.

Repeat this procedure for each of the other two sides of the triangle. When you are done, notice that the three perpendicular bisectors cross in a point. With metal point at that crossing and pencil at one of the corners of the triangle, draw a circle. Notice that it passes though each of the corners exactly, enclosing the triangle perfectly. The circle is called the circumcircle and its center is called the circumcenter. Mark the circumcenter C.

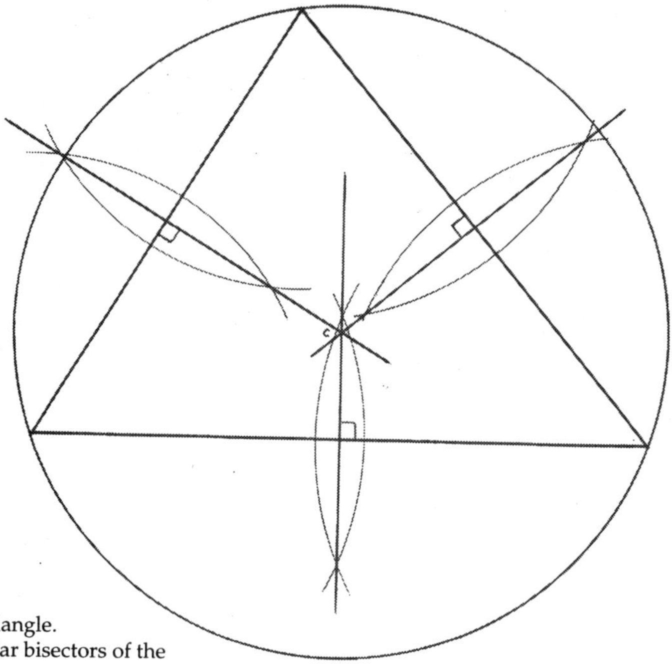

Fig. 9.
A scalene triangle.
Perpendicular bisectors of the sides, the circumcenter (C), and the circumcircle showing construction.

The circle is traditionally symbolic of the Divine. The circle envelops the triangle. The Divine Creator envelops your soul, protecting it.

Now lay this drawing over a clean sheet of paper and with the metal point of the compass poke through:

- the corners of the triangle,
- the midpoints of the sides,
- the circumcenter (C)

Using these poke holes as guides, draw the form again without construction arcs, and keep the perpendicular bisectors inside the triangle.

I did what he told me and it looks like this:

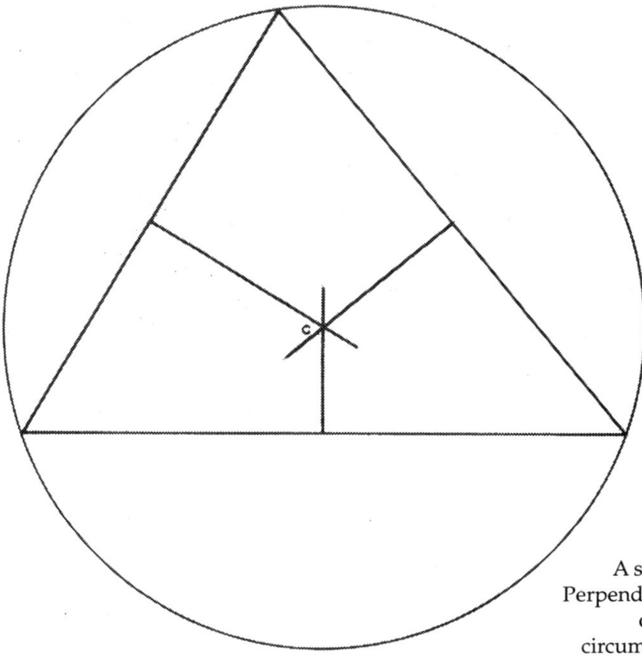

Fig. 10.
A scalene triangle.
Perpendicular bisectors of the sides, the circumcenter (C), and the circumcircle.

Good, he said. There is another center.

Another center? Two centers?

Yes. Lay your triangle, the one just completed, over another sheet of paper and with the metal point of the compass, poke through the same points as before:

- the three corners of the triangle,
- the midpoints of the sides,
- the circumcenter

Remove the top sheet and using the poke holes as guides, draw your triangle and mark the circumcenter C. Put a tiny dot at the midpoint of each side, (poke hole). You will need these later.

Select one corner of the triangle and with any convenient compass opening and metal point at that corner, draw an arc cutting the two sides of the triangle that meet in that corner. Mark those two points A and B. With metal point at A and any convenient compass opening, draw an arc. With metal point at B and the same compass opening, draw a second arc cutting the first one. Using a straightedge, draw a line from the corner of the triangle to the arc intersection. This line is called the angle bisector.

Fig. 11.
A scalene triangle.
An angle bisector.

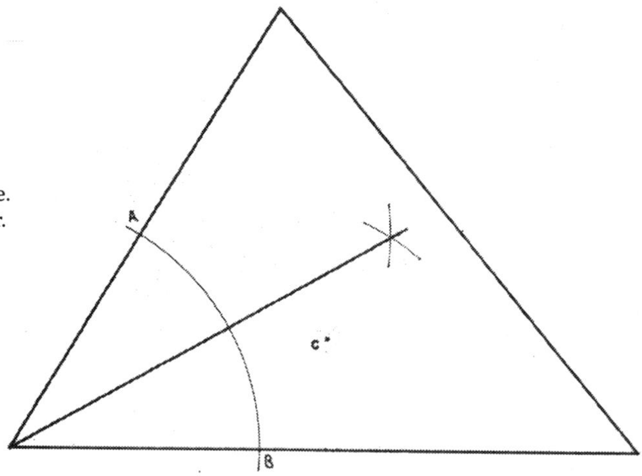

Repeat this procedure for each of the other two corners of the triangle. When you are done, notice that the three angle bisectors cross in a point. Notice also that this point is not at the same place as the circumcenter (C). With metal point at the crossing of angle bisectors, adjust the compass opening so that when you draw a circle, it exactly touches any one side of the triangle at one point. Notice that it exactly touches the other two sides also. This circle is called the inscribed circle and its center is called the incenter. Mark the incenter I.

I drew, and it came out like this. The angle bisectors crossed in a point, and the circle, with that point as center, touched the three sides.

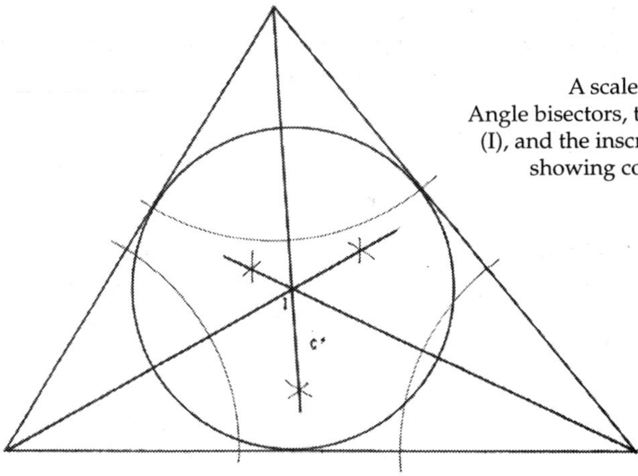

Fig. 12.
A scalene triangle.
Angle bisectors, the incenter (I), and the inscribed circle, showing construction.

Draw it again, he said, without construction arcs. Use the metal point of the compass and poke through this drawing onto a clean sheet:

- the corners of the triangle,
- the midpoints of the sides (to be used later),
- the circumcenter (C)
- the incenter (I)

Use the poke holes as a guide for your drawing.

I drew, and now it looks like this:

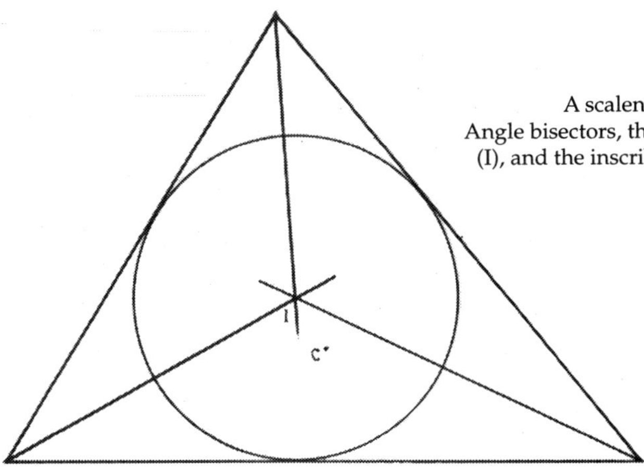

Fig. 13.
A scalene triangle.
Angle bisectors, the incenter (I), and the inscribed circle.

The circle, he continued, being symbolic of the Divine, now appears inside the triangle touching the three sides. The indwelling divine part of each human being touches the three soul capacities of thinking, feeling, and will such that, if desired, these soul capacities may be enhanced toward insightful thinking, compassion, and altruistic deeds.

I pondered this for a while.

Then he said, your triangle has yet another center.

Yet another center? I thought of a triangle as having one center. Now a third?

Yes. Lay the triangle you have just drawn over a clean sheet of paper and with the metal point of the compass, poke through:

- the three corners of the triangle,
- the midpoint of each side,
- the circumcenter (C)
- the incenter (I)

Remove the top sheet and using the poke holes as a guide, draw your triangle and mark the midpoints of each side, (poke holes) with a tiny dot. Mark also the circumcenter (C) and incenter (I). Using the straightedge, join each corner of the triangle to the midpoint of its opposite side. These lines are called medians.

I drew...

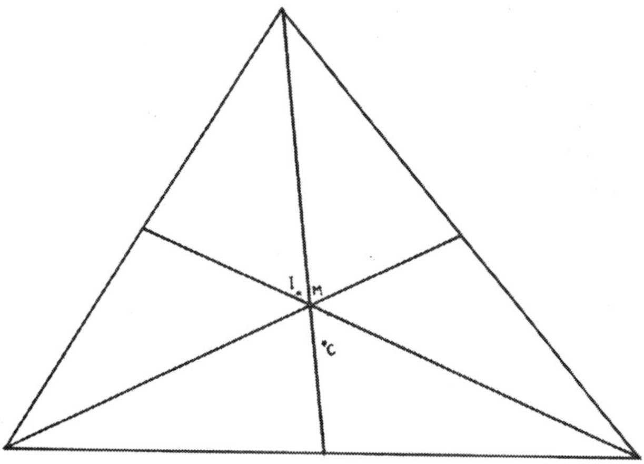

Fig. 14.
A scalene triangle.
Medians and the centroid (M).

and noticed that the three medians crossed in a point. Now, this point must be significant. The crossing of the perpendicular bisectors, and the crossing of the angle bisectors, each determined a significant point. But significant, how? I mused. I couldn't see how yet another circle could be drawn. A triangle has only corners and sides. One circle already touches the corners, and another already touches the sides. And the crossing of the medians is at a different location from the circumcenter (C) and the incenter (I).

You are wondering, he said, how the crossing of medians, which we call the centroid, can be significant. We shall soon see. But first mark the centroid M. (M for median intersection. We already have a point marked C). Now lay the triangle you have just drawn over a sheet of stiff paper. Poke through the three corners of the triangle and the centroid (M). Remove your drawing and using poke holes as guides, draw your triangle and put a tiny dot at the centroid. Carefully cut out the triangle and balance it at the centroid on a pencil point.

I found a used file folder and followed the instructions. Having drawn and cut very carefully, I balanced the triangle on the pencil point. Impressive.

Each one of us, he said, has a center of balance. That makes it possible for us to have learned to stand upright and walk at the age of about one year.

In spite of my initial incredulity, I had to agree that in the case of a triangle, there are in fact three centers. I was used to a circle having only one center, and a town having one center. Geometry can expand one's consciousness sometimes.

There is a fourth center of your triangle, he said.

A fourth center? Is the number of centers of a triangle infinite?

No. Once again, lay a clean sheet of paper under the triangle you drew last and with the metal point of the compass, poke through: the three corners of the triangle, the three centers already found, and the midpoints of the sides. Remove the top sheet and using the poke holes as guides, draw your triangle. Mark the three centers C, I, and M. Put tiny dots at the midpoints of the sides.

Now draw a perpendicular line from the top of the triangle straight down to the base–the side opposite the top corner. Here is how. With metal point at the top of the triangle, and any convenient compass opening, draw an arc that cuts the base in two places. Mark the two places A and B. You may have to extend the base line to the left and/or to the right. With metal point at A and any other convenient compass opening, draw an arc below the base. With metal point at B and the same compass opening, draw a second arc cutting the one just drawn. Lay the straightedge from the top of the triangle to the intersection of the two arcs below the triangle and draw a line. This line is called an altitude.

I drew and he watched.

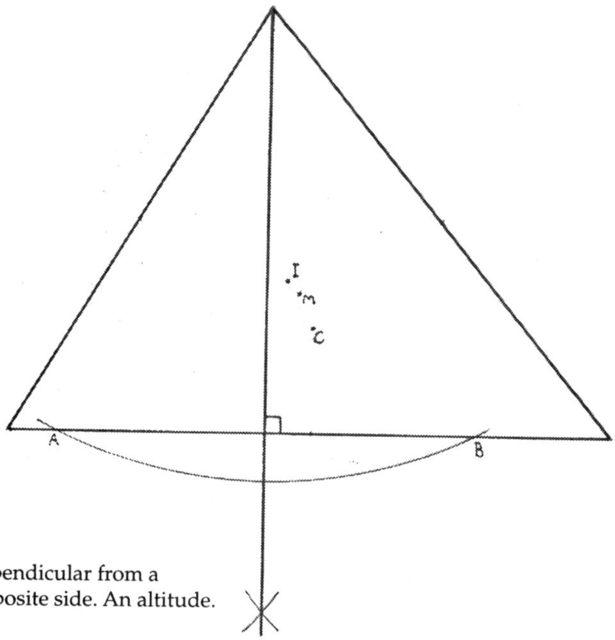

Fig. 15.
Dropping a perpendicular from a vertex to the opposite side. An altitude.

When I was done, he said, Good. Now, rotate the triangle so that another corner is at the top and another side is the base of the triangle and repeat the procedure. Do this a third time and make an observation.

I drew and saw that the three altitudes crossed in a point, and that this crossing was some distance away from the other three crossings; the circumcenter (C), the centroid (M), and the incenter (I). So I found the fourth center. But how can it be significant?

He looked at my drawing and said, Good.

Thank you.

The fourth center, he said, the crossing of altitudes is called the orthocenter. Mark it O on your drawing. You will soon see how it is significant. But first, make a drawing without construction arcs. Lay this drawing over a clean sheet of paper and with the metal point of the compass, poke through:

- the three corners of the triangle
- the four centers C, I, M, and O.

Using the poke holes as guides, draw the triangle with its altitudes but only the sections inside the triangle. Mark the four centers C, I, M, and O.

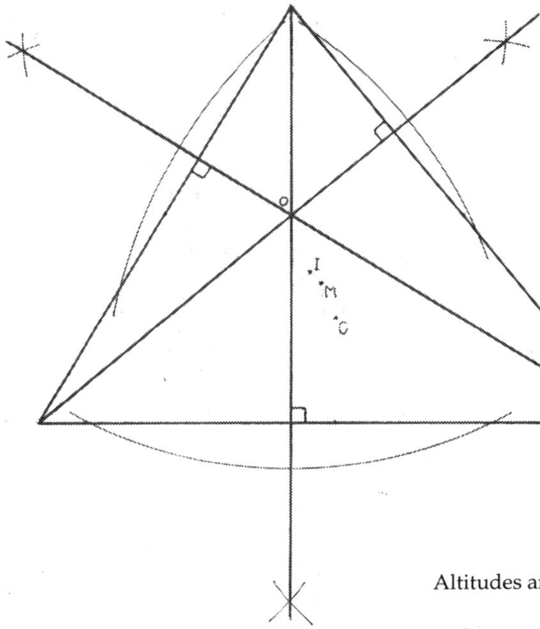

Fig. 16.
A scalene triangle.
Altitudes and the orthocenter (O).

Notice that the three altitudes that cross in the orthocenter are lines with one end at the corner of the triangle and the other end touching a point on that corner's opposite side making a right angle with that side. That point on the side of the triangle is called an altitude foot.

Join the three altitude feet with a straightedge and pencil to form a small triangle inside the large one. This small triangle, the altitude feet triangle, or pedal triangle, may be different from the larger triangle. Now with the metal point of the compass at the orthocenter (O), adjust the compass opening so that the circle you draw touches one side of the pedal triangle. Notice that the circle also touches the other two sides. What would you need, to find the center of an inscribed circle?

I rummaged through my collection of drawings and found the one I was looking for: Fig.12.

Why, of course, I said, you would need to draw angle bisectors. That was the second of the four centers we found. And because a circle has only one center, the orthocenter must also be the incenter of the inscribed circle of the pedal triangle.

I felt proud of my penetrating insight into geometrical matters.

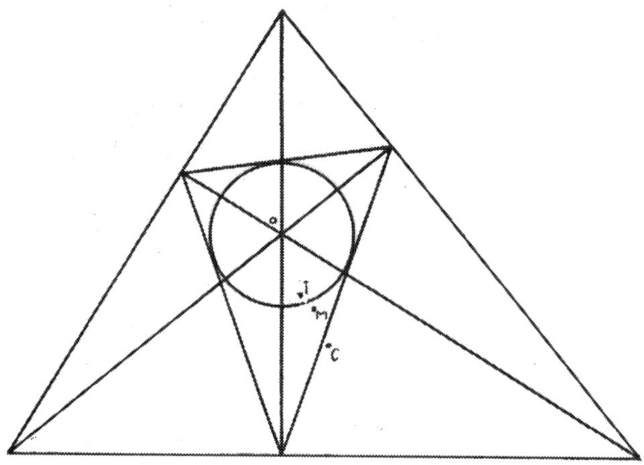

Fig. 17.
A scalene triangle with altitudes, the pedal triangle and its inscribed circle.

Good observation, he said. Now we have three circles connected with your triangle: the large one, the circumcircle, symbolic of the enveloping Divine, the smaller one, the inscribed circle, symbolic of the personal indwelling divine, and now the pedal triangle's inscribed circle, symbolic of the Divine working to develop the higher self to ever greater perfection.

On the drawing you have just completed, draw the inscribed circle of your triangle whose center is the incenter (I), and the circumscribed circle whose center is the circumcenter (C).

Or, if you prefer, draw a new triangle showing the three circles. Lay your drawing over a clean sheet of paper and with the metal point of the compass, poke through:

- the corners of the large triangle
- the altitude feet
- the orthocenter (O)
- the circumcenter (C)
- the incenter (I)

With poke holes as guides, draw:

- your triangle
- the pedal triangle and its inscribed circle whose center is the orthocenter
- the inscribed circle of your triangle whose center is the incenter (I)
- the circumscribed circle whose center is the circumcenter (C)

I drew and it looked like this:

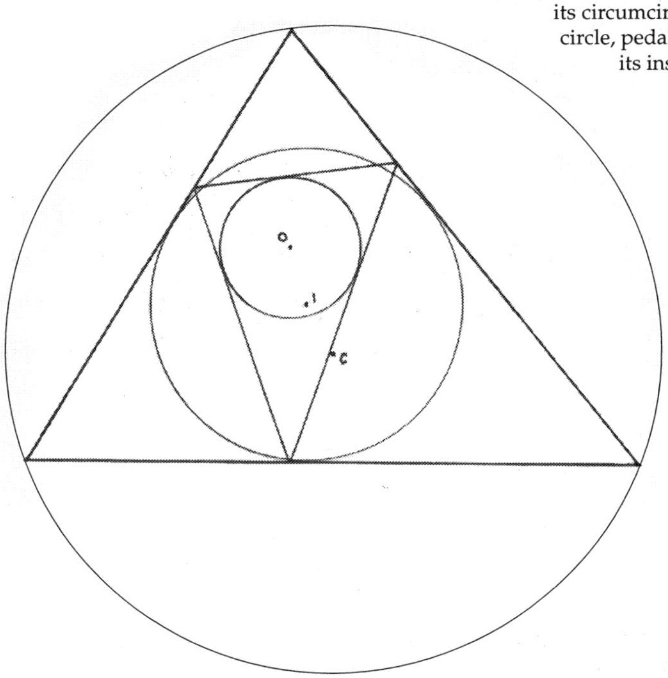

Fig. 18.
A scalene triangle with its circumcircle, inscribed circle, pedal triangle and its inscribed circle.

And yet, I thought, the symbolism of the three circles isn't easy to comprehend.

But now, I asked him, what if, as you said, without thinking, my hands had drawn a triangle in which the two sides were the same length, and the third side rather short.

Such a triangle, he said, would have symbolized the even development of two of your soul qualities, the third one still needing to be worked on. Draw an isosceles triangle. Find the four centers and make an observation.

How do I start?

Start by drawing a horizontal line any length to serve as a base, using the straightedge. Open the compass to a distance greater than the length of the line and with metal point at one end of the line, draw an arc above the line. With metal point at the other end of the line, and the same compass opening, draw an arc cutting the first one. Join the point at which the arcs cross to the ends of the line. You have an isosceles triangle in which two sides are equal and longer than the third.

I drew and it looked like this:

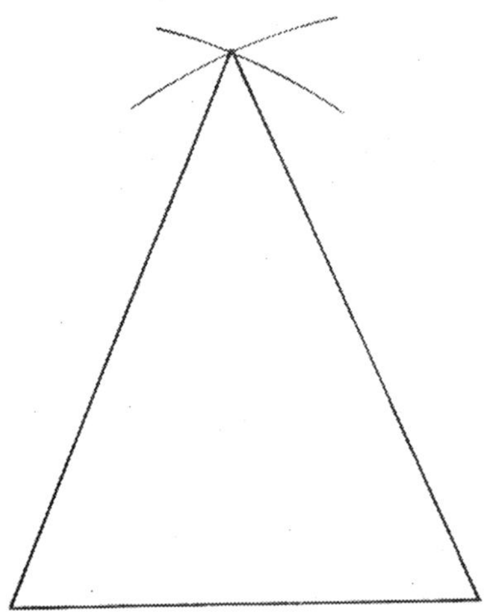

Fig. 19.
An isosceles triangle.

But, I asked, do the two equal sides have to be longer than the line I started with?

No, he said, they could be shorter. We will discuss that situation later.

On the isosceles triangle that you drew, he continued, draw:

- perpendicular bisectors of the sides and determine the circumcenter (C).
- angle bisectors and determine the incenter (I).
- medians and determine the centroid (M).
- altitudes and determine the orthocenter (O).

and while you are drawing, make an observation.

I needed to look back to Fig. 9, Fig. 12, Fig. 14, and Fig 16 to remind myself about constructions. Then I drew, watching for something that could be called an observation.

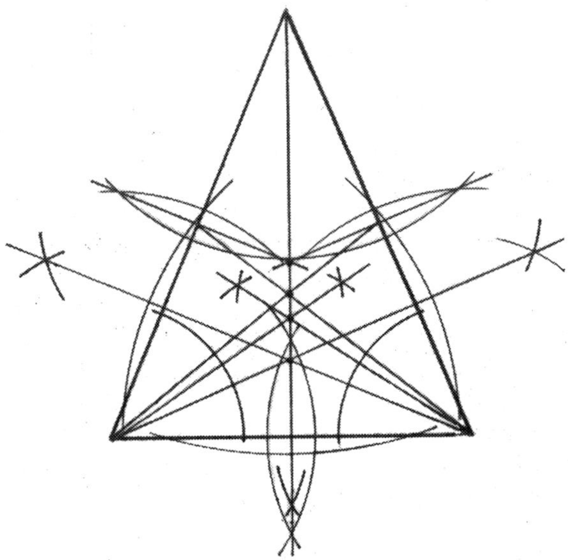

Fig. 20a.
The four centers of an isosceles triangle, showing construction.

Soon it became clear—well, clear to me. But anyone reading this may have a different view. I drew it again, (knowing by now how to poke through), leaving out the construction arcs.

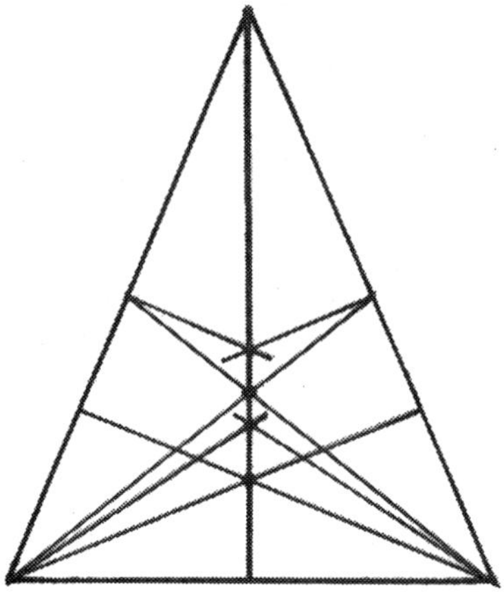

Fig. 20b.
The four centers of an isosceles triangle.

My observation: The vertical line, reaching from the top of the triangle to the midpoint of the base is at the same time the perpendicular bisector of the base, the bisector of the top angle, a median, and an altitude. And further, all four centers line up on that vertical line, in contrast to the seeming randomness in the way the centers are distributed in my original triangle. Neat.

Good, he said. The lining up of the centers symbolizes evidence of an inner order having developed as a result of efforts made to bring one of the less developed soul qualities up to the level of the more developed one. The vertical line being four lines at the same time, further indicates that an inner harmony has developed up to a point. Such people as this triangle symbolizes could be significant personalities in history or current events.

Would you be interested in exploring the various properties of a triangle with all three sides equal, an equilateral triangle?

Yes, certainly, I said. That would be most interesting. Because, in my triangle the lengths of the sides were all different and the centers were all scattered about inside. What if, by chance, without thinking, my hands had drawn an equilateral triangle?

That would likely not yet have happened, he replied, because your soul forces—your thinking capacity, feeling life, and will are not yet completely balanced. But let's draw an equilateral triangle and look for its centers.

First draw a horizontal line any length. Open the compass to the length of that line. With metal point at one end of the line draw an arc above the line. With the same compass opening and metal point at the other end of the line, draw an arc cutting the first one. Join the point at which the arcs cross with the ends of the original line. You now have an equilateral triangle.

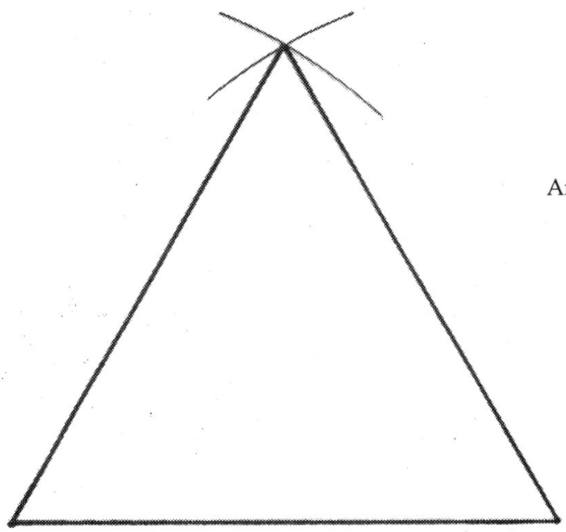

Fig. 21.
An equilateral triangle.

All on this equilateral triangle draw:

- perpendicular bisectors of the sides. Determine the circumcenter and draw the circumcircle.
- angle bisectors. Determine the incenter and draw the inscribed circle.
- medians and determine the centroid.
- altitudes. Determine the orthocenter and draw a pedal triangle and its inscribed circle.

While you are drawing, make some observations.

Again, I had to look back at Fig. 9, Fig. 12, Fig. 14, Fig 16, and Fig. 17 for construction reminders.

Your drawing, he said, will have many construction arcs which will make it look cluttered, perhaps. Lay it over a clean sheet of paper and with the metal point of the compass, poke through:

- the three corners of the triangle
- the midpoints of the sides
- the center(s).

Using poke holes as guides, redraw the triangle with its lines and circles leaving out construction arcs. When you are ready, you may want to speak about your observations.

I drew, and it took a while, and I could hardly wait to describe all my observations. Finally, the drawing was complete,

Fig. 22.
The equilateral triangle, its center and circles including its pedal triangle.

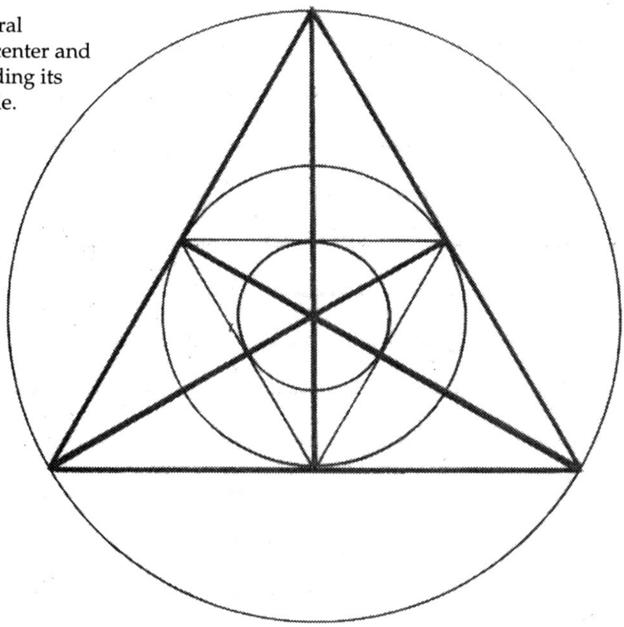

and I could say, I didn't have to draw everything. The perpendicular bisectors of the sides, the angle bisectors, the medians, and the altitudes are all the same. And all four centers meet in one center.

Good, he said. Compare the sizes of the three small triangles whose corners are the corners of the large triangle, and whose opposite sides are the sides of the pedal inner triangle.

Aha! I thought I had observed all that there was to observe that was worth mentioning. They are all the same size, four triangles the size of the pedal triangle. The large triangle is divided into four equal parts.

Now, he said, in your imagination, cut out the large triangle and fold the paper by bringing each corner of the large triangle to the midpoint of its opposite side. The fold lines will be the sides of the pedal triangle. Unfold. Fold again bringing the three corners of the large triangle together in a point, making a pyramid with a triangular base. This form is called a tetrahedron. It is one of the five Platonic solids. Plato and the medieval philosophers taught that it is symbolic of fire. But fire in the language of the soul is enthusiasm. Some people have a hard time understanding such symbolism.

I agreed that the symbolism wasn't easy but who am I to argue with Plato? Perhaps, one day I'll understand.

What you have cut and folded, he said, was in your imagination. Your triangle is still there. This time compare the sizes of the circles.

I used the compass opening needed to draw the smallest circle as the unit of measure and found the distance from triangle center to the middle circle to be exactly two units, and the distance from triangle center to the circumscribed circle to be exactly four units. Simple numerical relationships: 1,2,4. Each is double the one before. Symmetry, perfection, beauty.

Good observation, he said. Then he showed me a picture framed in an equilateral triangle of him who had perfected his soul qualities and balanced them with the help of the divinity within and enveloping him. He was then ready to teach, to offer his people guidelines for soul growth.

Fig. 23.
The Buddha.

You were right, I said, when I asked you, what if, by chance, without thinking, my hands had drawn an equilateral triangle? And you said that that would likely not yet have happened because my soul forces are not yet completely balanced. I guess it will be a while before I reach the stature of someone like Buddha. Perhaps never.

Don't let yourself get discouraged, he said. Others are waiting to help you, as Buddha helped his people.

Thank you. Is now a good time to discuss the isosceles triangle with shorter sides? You said we would discuss it later.

Yes, now is a good time. Draw an isosceles triangle. First, a horizontal line of any length, then with the metal point of the compass at one end of the line and compass opening a little greater then half the length of the line, draw an arc above the line. With the metal point at the other end of the line, and the same compass opening, draw another arc cutting the first one. Join the point at which the arcs cross with the ends of the line. You have then what is called an obtuse isosceles triangle. Obtuse, because one angle is greater than a right angle.

I drew and it looked like this:

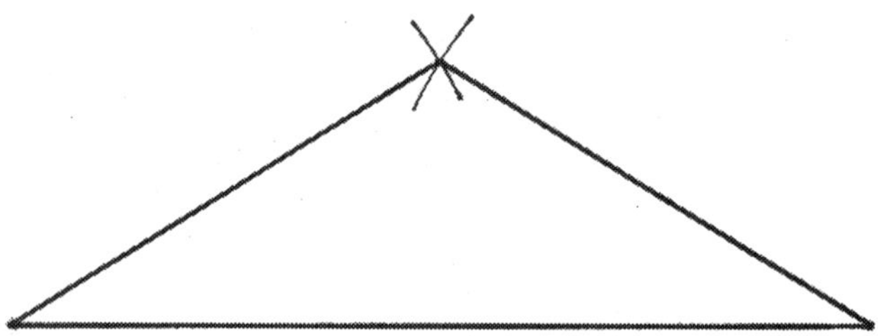

Fig. 24.
An obtuse isosceles triangle.

Good, he said. You could now proceed to find the four centers but this triangle is not symbolic of many people's soul development, two soul qualities lagging far behind a much stronger one, and the two weaker ones equally undeveloped. But we could consider a triangle whose three sides are different with one of them very long.

I drew another one.

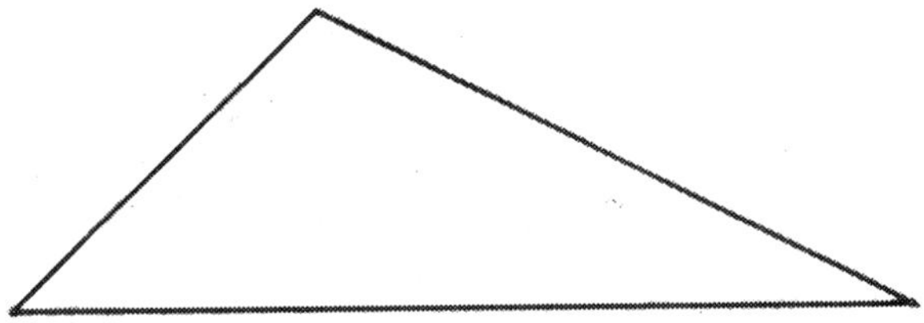

Fig. 25.
An obtuse scalene triangle.

Good, he said. Proceed as usual. All on the same triangle, draw:

–perpendicular bisectors of sides.

You will need to extend some of the sides of the triangle. But extensions are still part of the sides of a triangle. Get used to the idea that the three lines that form the triangle can be extended in both directions right across the page and beyond, and it is still the same triangle. Determine the circumcenter (C).

I looked back at Fig. 9, drew and found that the perpendicular bisectors of the sides are nowhere near each other.

Aha, I said. Observation number one: the obtuse triangle has no circumcenter.

Extend the bisectors, he said, beyond the borders of the triangle.

I extended them and they crossed in a point outside the triangle. Oops. Hasty conclusion. Maybe the short side of my triangle symbolizes my thinking capacity. Sorry. The observation should have been: The crossing of perpendicular bisectors of the sides is outside the triangle. But is that the circumcenter of a circumcircle? With the metal point of the compass at that supposed circumcenter (C) and pencil at one corner of the triangle, I drew a circle and it touched the other two sides. Nice.

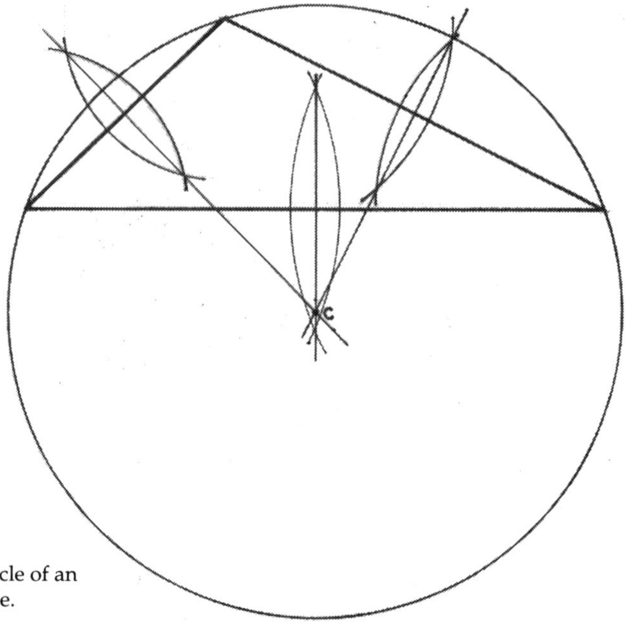

Fig. 26.
The circumcircle of an obtuse triangle.

The obtuse triangle, he said, may symbolize someone in a temporary state of emotional unbalance. Thinking isn't clear. Will is out of control, perhaps. When such a person recovers himself, his usual soul state is symbolized by a scalene triangle, maybe similar to yours. But notice that you can still draw a circle that symbolizes the enveloping divine.

Now, lay this drawing over a clean sheet of paper and poke through:

- the three corners of the triangle,
- the midpoints of the sides,
- the circumcenter (C)

Remove the top sheet and using the poke holes as guides, draw:

- the triangle
- the three perpendicular bisectors of the the sides,
- the circumcircle

Mark the circumcenter (C) without construction arcs. That way the next step will be easier.
Draw angle bisectors, determine the incenter (I) and draw the inscribed circle.

I pondered for a moment. Could the incenter (I) also be outside the circle? Hmm.... But I had better get on with the drawings. After refreshing my memory with Fig. 12, I drew and found the incenter (I) and the inscribed circle to be inside the triangle. Actually, I could have known that an inscribed circle could not be outside the triangle!

You are right, he said, Now draw medians and determine the centroid (M).

This time I didn't have to look back through my collection of drawings. I remembered that a median connects the midpoint of a side with the opposite corner of the triangle. That being the case, the center of balance, the centroid (M) would have to be inside the triangle. I drew and found my conjecture to be confirmed.

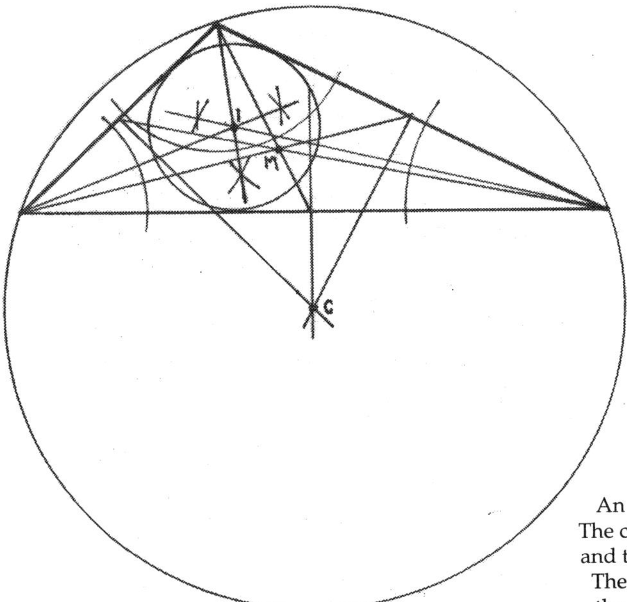

Fig. 27.
An obtuse triangle.
The circumcenter (C) and the circumcircle.
The incenter (I) and the inscribed circle.
The centroid (M).

Lay this drawing over a clean sheet of paper and with the metal point of the compass, poke through:

- the three corners of the triangle,
- the circumcenter (C),
- the incenter (I),
- the centroid (M).

Remove the top sheet and using the poke holes as guides, draw the triangle and mark the three centers C, I, and M. Extend the two sloping sides of the triangle beyond the top corner and draw altitudes. When you are done, make an observation.

I drew the vertical altitude first. No problem. Then as suggested, I extended the two sloping sides of the triangle. Drawing the other two altitudes, I found them to meet in a point some distance above the triangle. I marked it O for orthocenter.

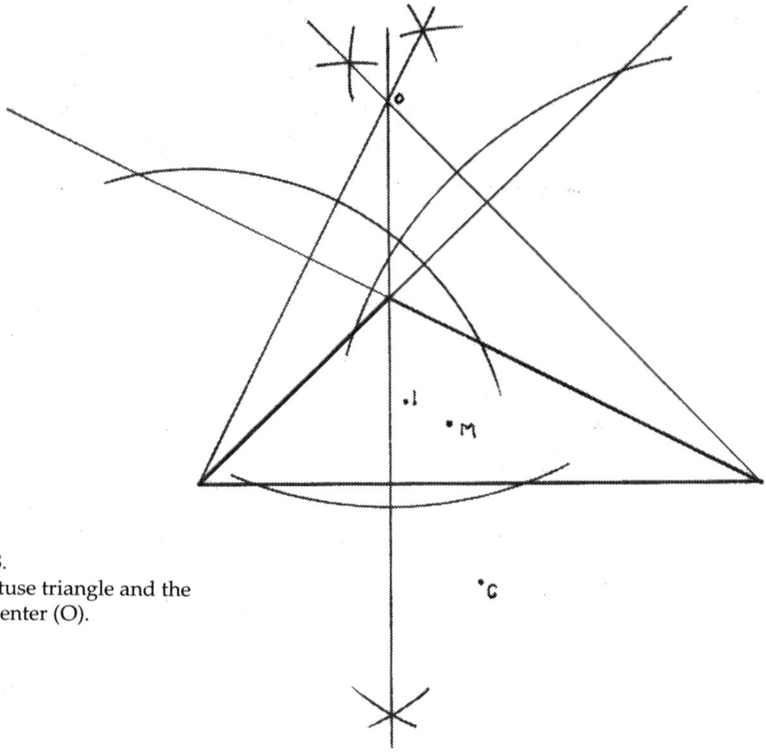

Fig. 28.
An obtuse triangle and the orthocenter (O).

Upon noticing that the four centers are spread out quite far, I mused that if the triangle were flatter, even more obtuse, the orthocenter and circumcenter would probably be located very far away from each other, even off the page, maybe.

Just to see, I drew an obtuse triangle with a very large angle, so that the triangle became quite flat in shape. I drew perpendicular bisectors of the sides and found the circumcenter to be located near the bottom of the page. I drew altitudes which I extended toward the top of the page. They would have met on a larger piece of paper quite far from the triangle. Now I could see that if the triangle were even flatter, the three altitudes would come close to being parallel. They would meet at a very great distance from the triangle. And the size of the inscribed circle would be very small. But even if the circumcenter

(C) were much farther from the triangle, I could see that the very large circumcircle would still pass through the three corners of the triangle. The circumcircle, being symbolic of the Divine, a personality which such a triangle symbolizes, should there be one, is still enveloped, protected by the Divine.

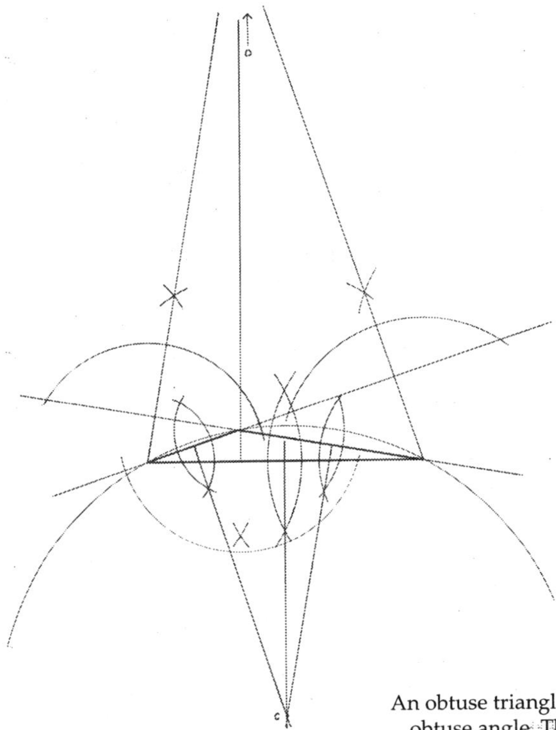

Fig. 29.
An obtuse triangle with a very large obtuse angle. The orthocenter and circumcenter.

Your thinking is correct, he said, but as I mentioned earlier, this triangle is symbolic of a temporary soul state, symbolic of someone who is momentarily uncentered, beside himself, perhaps with rage.

Thank you, I said. I hope never to be in such a state as that obtuse triangle symbolizes.

My eye was again drawn to the orthocenter and also to the location of the altitude feet. One of the altitude feet was on the base of the triangle. The other two were on the extensions of the other two sides of the triangle. I joined altitude feet. So here is what it looks like. Isn't the orthocenter supposed to be inside the pedal triangle to serve at the same time as center for the circle that touches its three sides?

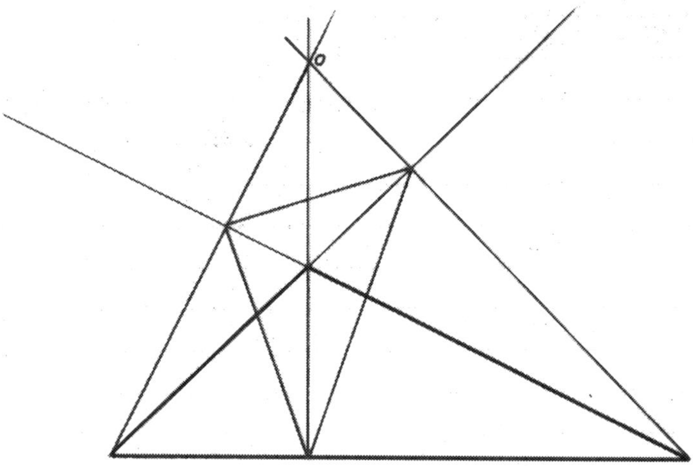

Fig. 30.
An obtuse triangle and its pedal triangle. The orthocenter.

From the point of view, he said, of your limited experience, yes. But the obtuse triangle has already demonstrated some features very different from what you have observed so far. Perhaps you could have expected one unusual feature to be followed by others. The center of the circle that touches the three sides of the pedal triangle is not the orthocenter. Can you find where that center is?

Guessing that the center ought to be somewhere there already, I put the metal point of the compass at the top corner of the obtuse triangle and adjusted the opening to touch one side of the pedal triangle. I drew a circle. It touched three sides. The center of the circle that touches the three sides of the pedal triangle is the corner of the obtuse triangle that make the obtuse angle. Bizarre! The orthocenter has been replaced by the corner of the triangle.

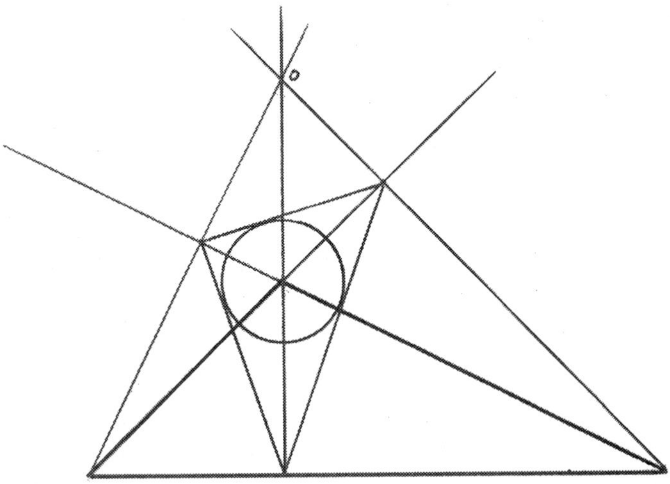

Fig. 31.
An obtuse triangle. The orthocenter, pedal triangle and its inscribed circle.

Good observation, he said. Look again at the drawing you have just completed. Visualize a scalene triangle formed by the base of the obtuse triangle as one side, and the other two sides, the altitudes in your drawing meeting at the orthocenter (O). If you were to draw altitudes in this new triangle, where would they be?

Hmm... One altitude would be the vertical one as before, and the other two would have to be the two sloping sides of the former obtuse triangle.

Good. Can you see that the altitude feet for the scalene triangle are at the same place as the altitude feet of your former obtuse triangle?

So they are. Astonishing!

And the pedal triangle is the same for both the imagined scalene triangle and the obtuse triangle you drew.

Yes, I see it now. The same pedal triangle for two different triangles. Who would have expected...?

They are different, yes, but they are closely related. Now, where is the orthocenter of the imagined scalene triangle?

Why, where it should be, in the center of the little circle, which is the same circle for both my obtuse triangle drawing and the imagined scalene triangle. But they would have to be the same, wouldn't they, because the pedal triangle is the same for both.

You are right, he said. If you hadn't drawn the obtuse triangle with heavy lines and marked the orthocenter (O), the two—the triangle you drew and the one you imagined—would be identical. They symbolize the same person, his soul state in a fit of rage, as in your drawing, and as he is normally as in the imagined drawing. I used the word "identical." Actually, circumcenter (C), incenter (I), and centroid (M), if plotted, would be in different locations for each triangle.

I understand, I said. It is still all quite amazing. Thank you. But there is one more triangle that I am anxious to explore with your help. It is the right triangle, the one with the square corner. It is not likely that I would have drawn such a triangle.

You are right, he said, but now draw one.

How do I start?

There are several ways to draw a right triangle. The easiest is to trace the corner of a sheet of paper for the two sides that form the right angle and then drew any sloping line for the third side. But a method that might interest you more is the following:

With the straightedge, draw a line across the page. With any compass opening, about 2½ inches will do, place the metal point somewhere on the line near the middle, and draw a half circle, cutting the line in two places. Erase the ends of the line beyond the half circle. Select any point on the half circle and with the straightedge, join it to the ends of the line. This triangle has now its right angle at the top. The side opposite the right angle, the base in this case, is called the hypotenuse.

I drew, and it looked like this.

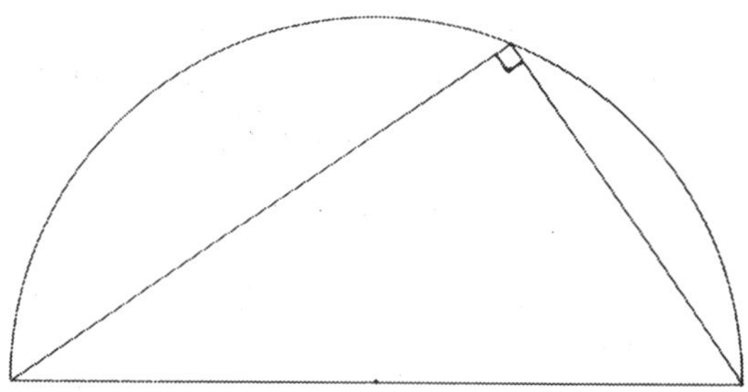

Fig. 32.
A right triangle in a semicircle.

I checked the accuracy of my right triangle drawing by putting the corner of a sheet of paper into the right angle on the half circle. It checked. The angle was a right angle. At the same time I puzzled over the statement, Select any point on the half circle... Any point? I picked several points and drew triangles, checked the angles at the half circle with the corner of a sheet of paper. They were all right angles. Astonishing. Then I showed him this one.

Good, he said. Now erase the half circle, determine the location of the circumcenter and the orthocenter, and make an observation.

Here we go again. First, the perpendicular bisectors of the sides. Soon I'll be able to do this in my sleep. Sleep!? All along, since the beginning of this adventure, it all seemed like a dream. Hmm.... But let's get on with the drawing. I drew and found the circumcenter to lie exactly where I had originally placed the metal point of the compass to draw a half circle (I did look back to FIg. 9 to verify my construction).

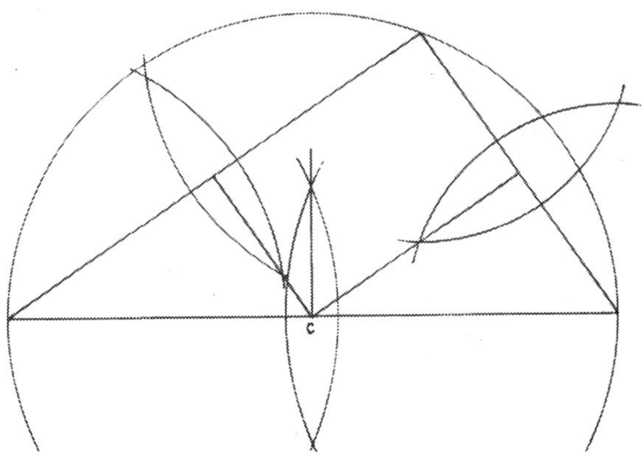

Fig. 33.
A right triangle.
Circumcenter (C) and circumcircle.

Observation number one: The circumcenter is the midpoint of the hypotenuse. Come to think of it, if I had drawn a complete circle instead of just a half circle at the beginning, the circumcircle would have been drawn, without perpendicular bisectors indicating where the circumcenter is located.

You have observed well, he said. Continue with the next part—the orthocenter.

He didn't ask me to locate the incenter and the centroid. But, of course, they would be somewhere inside the triangle. You can't draw a circle in a triangle unless the center of that circle is inside the triangle. And the center of balance has to be inside the triangle, too. Perhaps the orthocenter is another surprise. I began to draw and soon noticed that the two short sides of the right triangle needed to be extended, to draw the arcs. When I was done, it looked like this. You can see that, to avoid clutter, I drew the triangle again, this time without the perpendicular bisectors of the sides and their construction arcs. Not wanting him to see me make a silly mistake, I took a quick look at Fig. 16 to check my construction.

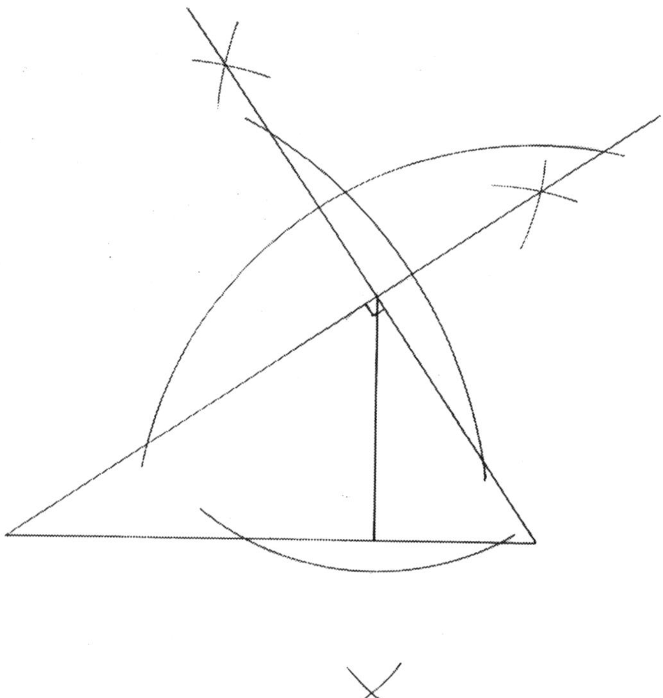

Fig. 34.
A right triangle with altitudes. Two of the three are sides of the triangle.

As I was drawing, I noticed that the vertical altitude was no surprise. But the other two altitudes were. They lined up exactly with the two short sides of the right triangle.

Good observation, he said. Now make an observation about the pedal triangle.

I looked at the drawing for a time. Is it possible? There is no pedal triangle. One altitude foot is on the base of the right triangle, on the hypotenuse, and the other two are both at the right angle. Joining them all we have a straight line.

You are right, he said. There are few people whose soul life is symbolized by a right triangle. Such a person has one soul quality strongly developed in contrast to the other two. Perhaps he is over-intellectual. But there is some inflexibility, some inability to adapt to varying circumstances. Having a right triangle as symbol of his soul life, he might insist that his way is right, even if times have changed. The square corner implies a "square" personality (if I may use a slang expression). He is old fashioned. The slightest change in the length of one or the other short side would separate the two altitude feet that were one, making an pedal triangle possible, and also its inscribed circle. Of course the inscribed circle of the right triangle is still possible. This personality needs only small change in one of the soul qualities, perhaps the feeling life, to become more human, more able to get along with others. The circumcenter and the orthocenter are not inside the triangle. Nor are they outside. The condition is not that of an obtuse triangle.

But moving on, he said, we need to concern ourselves with three more circles that are connected to your triangle.

Three more circles? We already have three—the circumscribed circle, the inscribed circle, and the little inscribed circle of the pedal triangle. Three more?

Yes, he said. These other three circles also touch the three sides of the triangle as does the inscribed circle, but in a different way.

Should I be surprised that there are more surprises?

You will need to bisect angles, he said. Do you remember how? It's been a while. Here is a reminder.

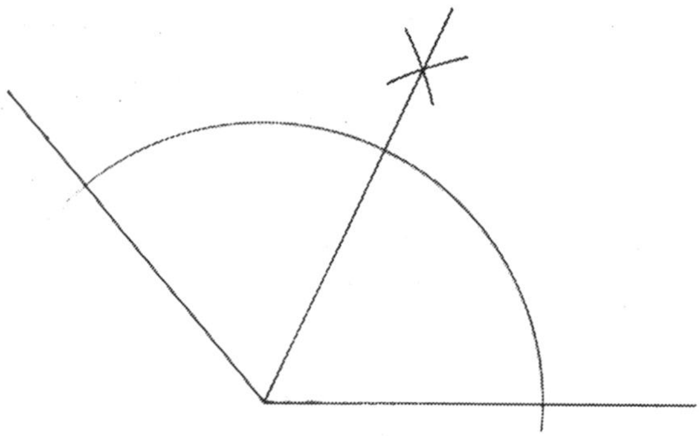

Fig. 35.
Bisecting an obtuse angle.

Thank you. It saves me rummaging through all my papers.

Draw your scalene triangle again, he said, this time somewhat smaller—a distant view, if you like. Extend the sides in both directions right across the page. Number the six obtuse external angles, and bisect angle 1.

I drew but I had to ask for help identifying the six obtuse external angles. Then I bisected angle 1.

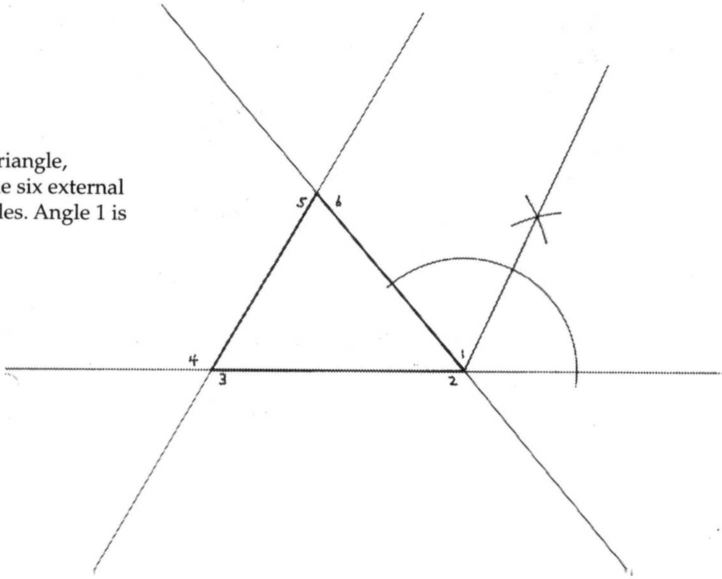

Fig. 36.
A scalene triangle, showing the six external obtuse angles. Angle 1 is bisected.

Good, he said. Now bisect angle 6 and extend, if necessary, the bisectors of angle 1 and angle 6 so that they cross. Place the compass point at the crossing of the angle bisectors and adjust the opening so that a circle just touches the side of the triangle between angles 1 and 6. This circle is called an escribed circle. Does this escribed circle also touch the extensions of the other two sides?

Why, yes, I exclaimed. I never would have thought that a circle other than the inscribed circle of a triangle could touch all three sides.

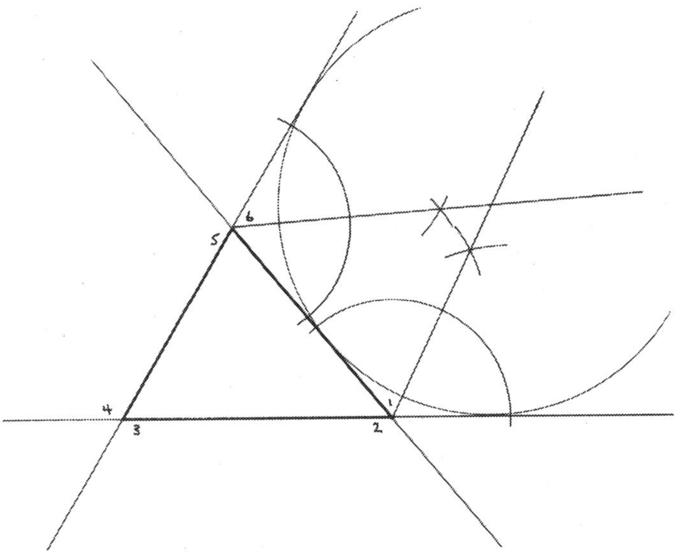

Fig. 37.
A scalene triangle.
External angles 1
and 6 are bisected to
determine the center
of one of the escribed
circles.

Without being told, I guessed that I was to repeat this procedure and draw the other two escribed circles. He nodded, so I bisected angles 2 and 3 and drew the second one, then I bisected angles 4 and 5 and drew the third one. Because the drawing looked cluttered with all the construction arcs and lines, I made a copy omitting them. And here it is—the three escribed circles of a scalene triangle.

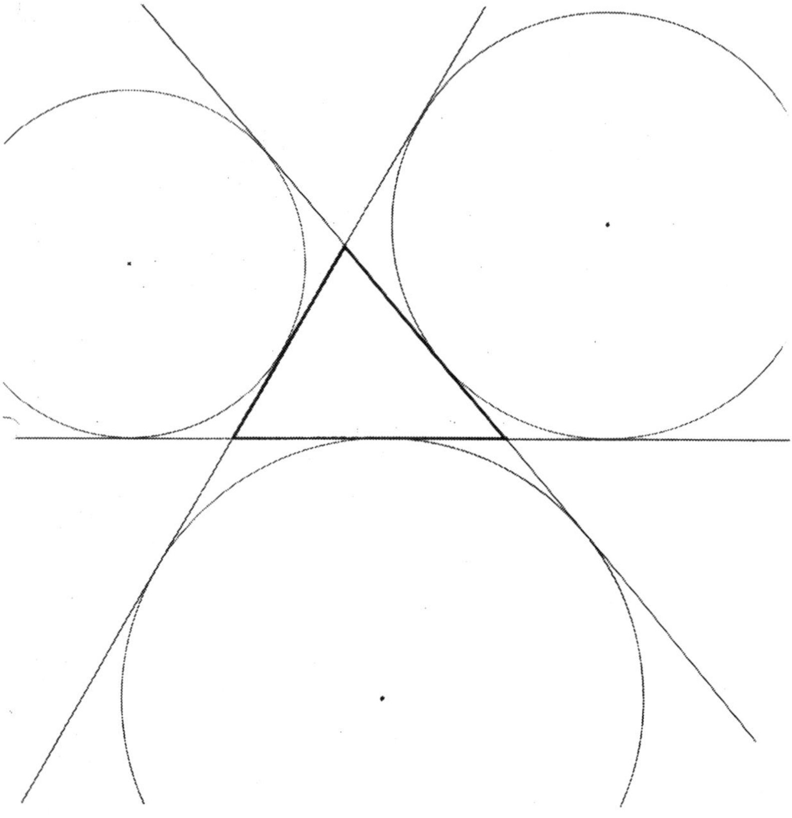

Fig. 38.
A scalene triangle and its
escribed circles.

Good, he said. Can you imagine what these three escribed circles might symbolize?

I understand, I said, that the circle is symbolic of the Divine. A circumcircle symbolizes the enveloping Divine. The inscribed circle symbolizes the indwelling Divine, and the little circle in the pedal triangle symbolizes the divine part of my higher self. But that little circle must be on a higher level, I would think. Regarding the three escribed circles, I don't know.

You are right, he said, about the Divine worlds having several levels. But a lower self and a higher self cannot easily be drawn on a sheet of paper. The Divine worlds have different levels and also different regions. Someone inspired to good deeds is in touch with one region. Another inspired artistically is touch with another region. So, St. Francis and Mozart were each inspired by different regions of the Divine worlds at moments when they were most active in whatever they became famous for. One region of the Divine worlds touches one soul capacity directly and the others as well but less directly. An escribed circle touches one side of the triangle directly, and the other two less directly in that it touches their extensions.

It's overwhelming, I said. Geometry should be spelt with a capital G.

Perhaps so, he replied, if it is a chapter out of the Book of Sacred Geometry. But now that you have learned how to draw the escribed circles to your scalene triangle, it should be possible to draw three escribed circles to its pedal triangle.

I suppose so, I responded. One should be able to draw escribed circles to any triangle.

But while I was saying this I was somewhat dazzled by the idea of yet another three circles connected with my scalene triangle. Soon I will lose count.

Draw, he said, and make an observation.

I copied my original scalene triangle with its pedal triangle, Fig. 17, and began to draw escribed circles, not expecting anything unusual. First I extended the sides of the pedal triangle. Then I began to bisect the external angles, and lo, the bisectors were already there, as sides of my scalene triangle. And the centers of the escribed circles were also already there, as corners of my scalene triangle. Who would have thought...? Everything is connected! I erased the arcs needed to draw the angle bisectors so as to avoid a cluttered looking drawing, and here it is:

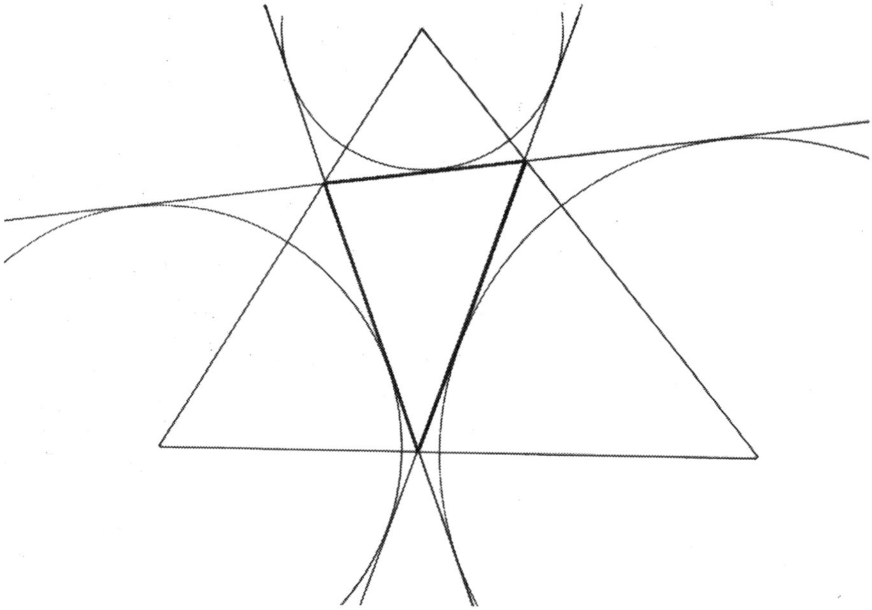

Fig. 39.
A scalene triangle and the escribed circles of its pedal triangle.

Yes, he said, everything is connected. You have observed well. Having now become acquainted with escribed circles, look back at your drawing of the obtuse triangle with its pedal triangle and its external orthocenter.

I rummaged through my papers and found the drawing. It was Fig. 28.

Copy that drawing by poking through on to a clean sheet of paper the:

- corners of the obtuse triangle
- orthocenter
- altitude feet.

Then using poke holes as guides, draw the obtuse triangle, the three altitudes, and the pedal triangle with sides extended. Add to your drawing the three escribed circles of the pedal triangle and make an observation.

I drew first the lower right escribed circle, knowing that its center was the corner of the triangle, then the lower left escribed circle. Then, taking a chance, I put the compass metal point at the orthocenter and drew a circle that touched the third side of the pedal triangle. And it touched the extensions of the other two sides! Beautiful! Everything is connected.

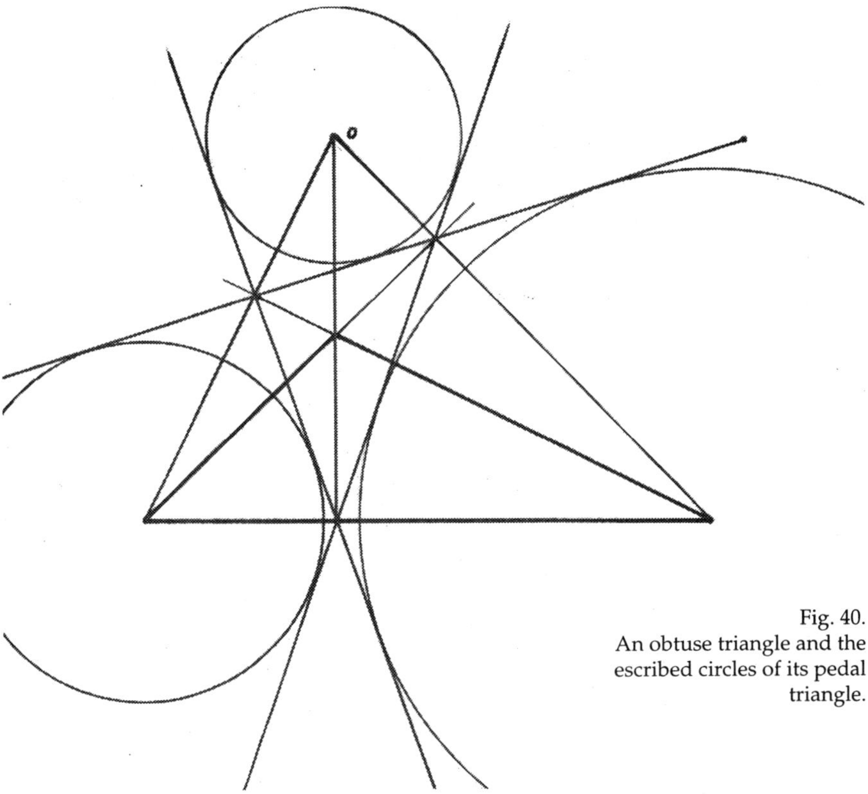

Fig. 40.
An obtuse triangle and the escribed circles of its pedal triangle.

Everything is connected, he echoed my comment again, and there are more connections. There is also another circle connected with a triangle.

Is it possible...? After having found the escribed circles, I assumed that finally we had exhausted the number of circles. But they all made sense so far. Maybe this new one will also be meaningful.

Draw a triangle, he said, similar to your original triangle, but a little smaller. I suggest a base of about 3½ inches long. Open the compass to about 3 inches and with metal point at one end of the line, draw an arc. Then with the compass opening about 2½ inches and metal point at the other end of the line, draw an arc cutting the first one. Join the point at which the arcs cross to the ends of the 3½ inch line, and there you are. The measurements need not be exact.

- Draw perpendicular bisectors of the sides and mark the circumcenter (C).
- Draw angle bisectors and mark the incenter (I).
- Draw medians and mark the centroid (M).
- Draw altitudes and mark the orthocenter (O).

Using the straightedge, draw a line from the circumcenter (C) to the orthocenter (O) and make an observation.

I drew. You, the reader of this adventure, drawing the figures, might want to be reminded about constructions. Look up Fig. 9, Fig. 12, Fig. 14, and Fig. 16.

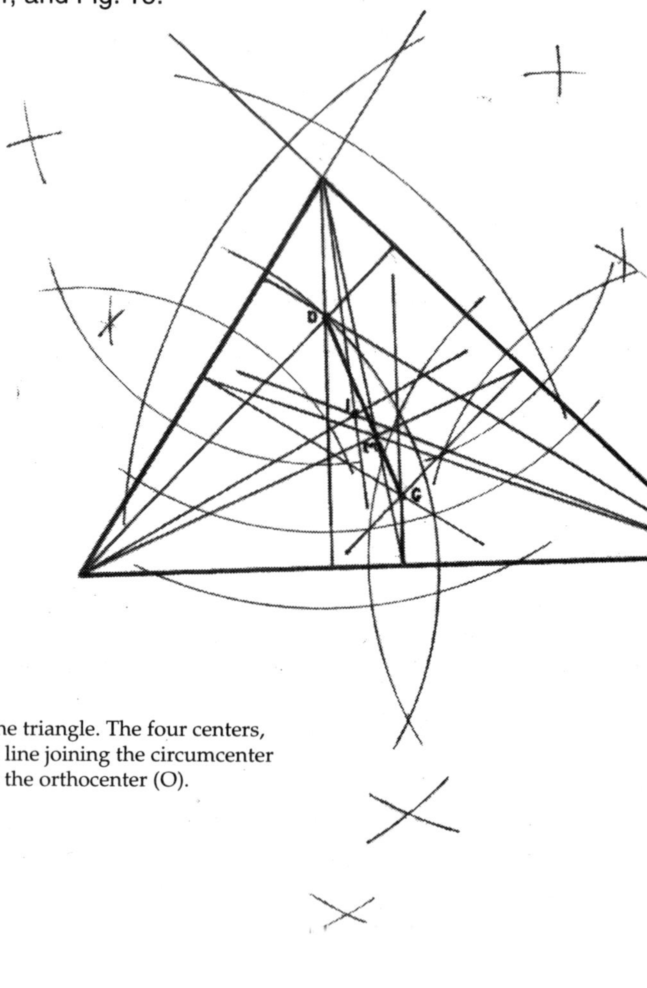

Fig. 41.
A scalene triangle. The four centers, and the line joining the circumcenter (C) and the orthocenter (O).

There was, in fact, a significant observation to be made. The four centers which seemed to me to be randomly distributed within the triangle were not. The circumcenter (C), centroid (M), and orthocenter (O) lay on a straight line. The incenter (I) was a little to one side. It appeared not to belong. Pity.

Good so far, he said. Find the midpoint of that CO line and with the metal point of the compass at that midpoint, and pencil at the midpoint of one of the sides of the triangle, draw a circle and make an observation.

I drew the same figure again, using the "poke hole" method, but leaving out the construction arcs.

I could have found the midpoint of that CO line in the way I began to draw perpendicular bisectors of the sides, but instead, because there were so many lines in the triangle, I just used a ruler with fine gradations, measured and divided by two. I drew the circle as directed. Surprise! The circle passed through the three midpoints of the sides and through the three altitude feet. It's a six-point circle!

Good, he said, but notice where that circle crosses the altitudes.

It took me a long time puzzling over this one, but suddenly, I thought I saw the circle crossing one of the altitudes maybe half way between orthocenter and triangle corner. I measured and sure enough, each of the three altitudes were crossed at the same place—at the midpoint between orthocenter and triangle corner. Now it's a nine-point circle!

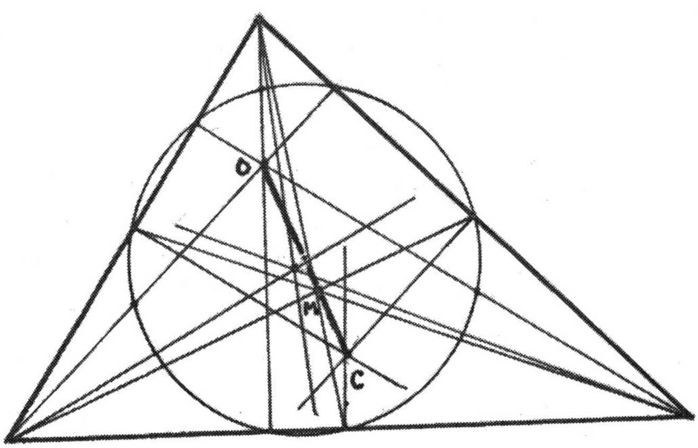

Fig. 42.
A scalene triangle.
The nine-point circle.

Very good, he said. You are becoming more and more observant. Draw the inscribed circle and the three escribed circles.

I drew. Surprise again! This inscribed circle just touched the nine-point circle in one place. So, the incenter, not lying on the line joining the circumcenter and the orthocenter is after all connected with the nine-point circle but in a different way.

I reminded myself of the escribed circle construction by looking back at Fig. 37, And then I saw that each of the escribed circles also touched the nine-point circle in one place. Now it's a thirteen point circle! I erased all the constructions arcs and here is the final result.

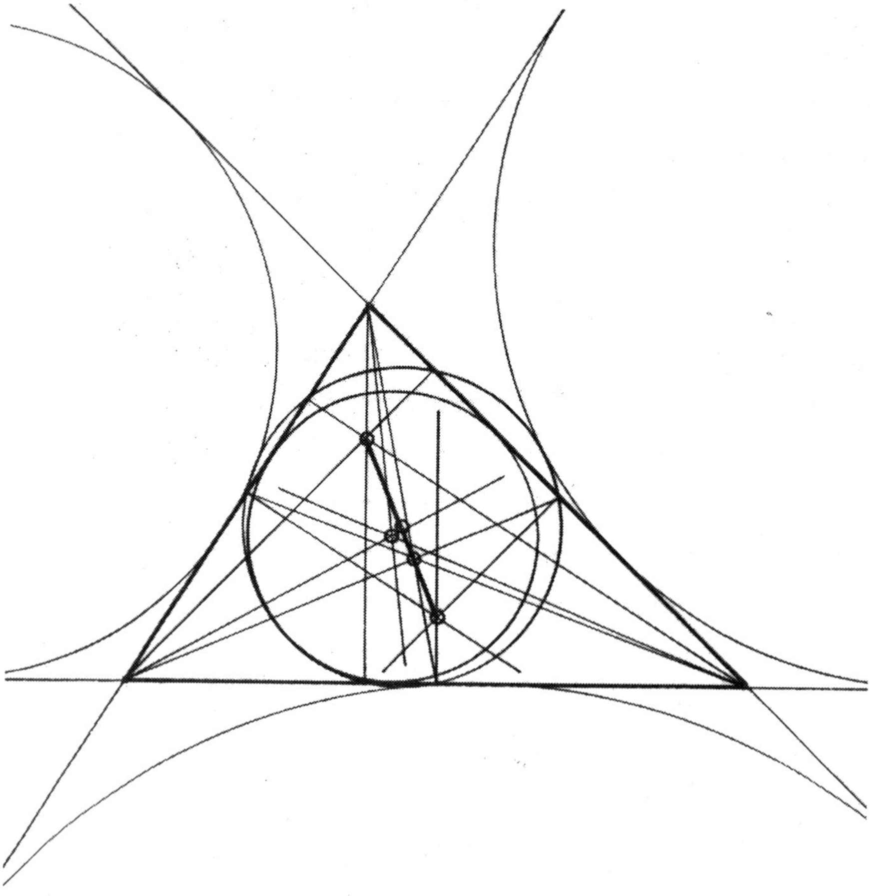

Fig. 43.
The thirteen-point circle

Good, he said. Very good. What can you make of the thirteen-point circle? Does what we have been doing so far lead you to imagine the symbolism in this drawing? Ponder for a moment and....

The alarm rang, I woke up. Time to get dressed, eat breakfast and go to work. But it was hard to concentrate on my work that day. Everything is connected. All the regions of the Divine worlds find expression in an orderly way in and around my soul life, even though I am far from perfection.

I must write it all down before I forget any part of it. And draw all those diagrams. If I draw first, the writing that goes with the drawings will come to mind. So, I sat down after I came home form work and drew. And when I was done, I heard a voice, I was sure I heard a voice.

Good, he said, very good.